Alkaline Diet
Cookbook
Volume 1
By Anas Malla

Bonus!! FREE E-Book

This great book has a Bonus E-book called "10.5 Tips for Massive Success". You can download the book from my website.

I am honored and grateful to give you this free e-book, and I hope this will really help you to start your ketogenic diet, you can easy read it after downloading.

Thank you and enjoy reading.

If the links do not work, for whatever reason, you can simply visit my website:

Mastering-life.com/10successtipsbook

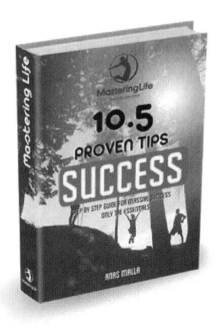

Table of Contents

Introduction

Let me thank you and congratulate for purchasing the **"Alkaline Diet Cookbook V.1"**

This book contains exactly 40 incredible recipes that perfectly fit with an alkaline diet.

All of the recipes are personally tested and the selected ones are my favorites. Each of them is extremely healthy and benefits to your overall health and well-being. They all keep in mind the famous 80:20 ratio that is the base of the alkaline diet.

The recipes are divided into several categories for your convenience:

- **Breakfast** – the ideal meals to get a jumpstart for the day
- **Smoothies** – an integral part of alkaline diet perfect to provide you with a boost of energy at any given time
- **Salads** – refreshing, healthy and completely alkaline meals that will delight you
- **Soups** – unique and carefully selected soups for all tastes
- **Entrees** – main courses that fit into alkaline diet

- **Desserts** – if you feel like it's time to indulge your sweet tooth, take a look here
- **Snacks** – are you looking for a quick snack to satisfy your hunger until dinner? Here are the ones carefully selected for you

The best alkaline recipes are in this cookbook, and there is no need for you to look anywhere else.

Thanks again for purchasing this book, I hope you enjoy reading it!

Breakfast

Quinoa Porridge
Serves 2

Ingredients

1 vanilla essence

½ lemon zest, grated

½ cup coconut milk (alternatively, you can use coconut cream)

½ teaspoon ground nutmeg

½ teaspoon of cinnamon (or 1 stick)

1 cup organic quinoa, dry

1 ½ teaspoons ground ginger

1 teaspoon ground cloves

2 cups of alkaline water (or pure)

A handful of nuts and seeds for garnish

Directions

1. Check the package instructions and prepare the quinoa in accordance with them. Make sure that you drain it after cooking.
2. Use a saucepan and add drained quinoa to it. Also add ground cloves, ground nutmeg, ground ginger, and cinnamon. Stir the ingredients well to combine.
3. Add coconut milk (or cream) and vanilla essence. Stir everything to combine the ingredients. Once you heat everything and properly combine the ingredients, transfer them to a serving bowl.
4. Sprinkle with a handful of nuts and seeds of your choice and garnish. You can drink coconut yogurt with quinoa porridge.

Bean Quinoa Bowl
Serves 2

Ingredients

1 cup quinoa

3 green onions, sliced

4 cloves of garlic, minced

2 avocados, sliced

2 cans Adzuki beans (30 ounces in total)

2 limes, juiced

1 teaspoon cumin

A handful of chopped cilantro

Directions

1. Use a pot and add quinoa to it along with 2 cups of water. Boil everything and cover the pan once it comes to a boil. Turn the heat down and allow it to sit on the stove for about 45 minutes.
2. In the meantime, rinse the cans of Adzuki beans and add them to a small saucepan. Place it on a stove over low temperature and add lime juice, cumin, garlic, and onions. Stir the ingredients to mix them and allow it to simmer for about 15 minutes so that the flavors can combine.
3. Once quinoa is cooked, drain it and transfer it to serving bowls proportionally. Top with the bean mixture (make sure to also distribute it equally) and add sliced avocado to it. Use cilantro for garnish and serve.

Chopped Blueberries with Coco Butter and Mint
Serves 1

Ingredients

1 cup of blueberries (you can also use raspberries or strawberries or combine them altogether)

1 tablespoon mint, chopped

2 tablespoons coconut butter, melted

Directions

1. Wash the berries and place them in a serving bowl. Melt the coconut butter over the stove or in your microwave (don't forget to use a heat-proof dish in that case).
2. Use the melted butter to drizzle the berries. Next, use mint to sprinkle the mixture and serve immediately.

Alkaline Muesli
Serves 1

Ingredients

1 cup coconut milk, unsweetened (you can use almond milk instead)

1 tablespoon almonds, sliced

½ cup apple, chopped

½ cup rolled oats, gluten-free

A dash of cinnamon

Directions

1. Use a serving bowl and add unsweetened coconut milk and rolled oats in it. Cut the apples and slice the almonds and throw them into the mixture, as well as a dash of cinnamon. Combine everything if to mix the ingredients.
2. Place the oats in the fridge for at least an hour to soak (you can also soak them the night before).

Tip: If you prefer hot muesli, cook the oats on the stove before throwing in almonds and apples.

Smoothies

Green Power Smoothies
Serves 1

Ingredients

2 tomatoes

1 cucumber

A handful spinach leaves

1 avocado

½ red pepper

1 lime

½ teaspoon vegetable stock

Directions

1. Make sure to wash all the ingredients carefully. Use a knife to chop tomato, cucumber, avocado, and pepper into pieces.
2. Use a cup and add ¼ cup of warm water to it along with the vegetable stock. That will help the stock to dissolve.
3. Add the stock and avocado to a blender or a food processor and process until you get a pasty consistency. Add cucumber, tomatoes, and red pepper to the blender and process once again. This time you are aiming to get a consistency that has more liquid.
4. Finally, add lime and spinach to the mix and combine everything. You want to correctly process the ingredients and get a smoothie-like consistency.
5. Transfer to a tall glass and serve.

Prevent Reflux Smoothie
Serves 2

Ingredients

1 teaspoon ground ginger

1 teaspoon nutmeg

1 teaspoon cardamom

1 teaspoon ground cinnamon

1 bag of loose leaf tea of your choice

1 tablespoon coconut oil

1 tablespoon chia seeds

1 cup unsweetened almond milk (you can use coconut milk instead)

1 cup coconut cream

½ avocado, sliced

A handful of walnuts

A handful of almonds

A handful of bok choi or kale

Directions

1. Place a saucepan on the stove and adjust the temperature to very low. Add almond milk, coconut cream, ground ginger, ground cinnamon, nutmeg, and cardamom to it. Finally, add the tea bag (or leaves). Combine everything to mix the ingredients and bring it to simmer. Allow it to sit on the stove for about 5 minutes. You don't have to spend that much time to infuse the flavors, but if you want them truly infused, be patient.

2. Once you sense the amazing flavor from the mixture, transfer it to a high-speed blender and take out the tea bag (or leaves). Add sliced avocado, coconut oil, walnuts, almonds, bok choi or kale, and chia seeds to the blender. Process the ingredients until you get a smooth consistency (you can make a couple of pauses to stir the ingredients a bit).

3. You can add some ice or place to a smoothie in the fridge to cool it down before serving.

Healthy Alkaline Smoothie
Serves 2

Ingredients

1 avocado

1 cup coconut water

A piece of turmeric, freshly grated

A piece of ginger, freshly grated

A handful or arugula (or rocket or watercress)

A handful of coriander (or parsley)

A handful of baby spinach

A pinch of cayenne

½ capsicum

A pinch of salt

Directions

1. Add all the root vegetables into a high-speed blender along with coconut water (you can use pure instead) and sliced avocado. Blend everything to combine the ingredients.
2. Add the remaining things from the list of the ingredients and blend once again until you get a smooth consistency.
3. You can add some ice or place a smoothie in the fridge to cool it down before serving.

Super Immunity Juice
Serves 2

Ingredients

1 garlic clove

1 celery stalk

1 cucumber

1/2 inch turmeric, raw

1/2 inch ginger raw

1/2 lemon juice

2 tomatoes

Directions

1. Use a juicer to juice cucumber, tomatoes, celery stalk, lemon, garlic, ginger, and turmeric. Stir to combine the ingredients well and serve immediately.
2. You can add some ice or place a smoothie in the fridge to cool it down before serving.
3. Tip: Make sure to immediately wash your juices after you are done with making this recipe. Otherwise, you are risking that all the juices you make in the near future have a garlic hint.

Energizing Smoothie
Serves 2

Ingredients

½ avocado, sliced

½ cucumber

1 tablespoon chia seeds

1 tablespoon sunflower seeds

¼ cup almonds, soaked

1/8 cup cashews, soaked

A handful of kale

2 handfuls of spinach leaves

1 cup almond milk

3 tablespoons coconut oil

Directions

1. The first thing you need to do is to soak your cashews and almonds in a bit of water. You should allow them to soak for at least an hour (if you are in a hurry, 20 minutes will do, but it won't have the same flavor). You can also do the soaking the night before and leave it in the fridge overnight.
2. Slice the avocado and add it to the blender along with the cucumber and almond milk. Process everything to combine the ingredients well.
3. Next, add spinach leaves, kale, and coconut oil. Process once again to blend the ingredients.
4. Add the soaked cashews and almonds, as well as sunflower seeds and chia seeds to the blender. Process everything once again until you get a smooth consistency.
5. You can add some ice or place to a smoothie in the fridge to cool it down before serving.

Ultimate Blueberry Smoothie
Serves 1

Ingredients

½ cup blueberries

1 cup coconut milk (you can use almond milk instead)

1 tablespoon chia seeds

1 tablespoon almond butter, raw

1 tablespoon flaxseed, ground

1 tablespoon coconut oil

1 tablespoon hemp seed powder

A handful of spinach leaves

Directions

1. Use a high-speed blender and add blueberries, coconut milk, chia seeds, almond butter, ground flaxseed, coconut oil, hemp seed powder, and spinach leaves to it. Process everything until you get a smooth consistency.
2. You can add some ice or place the smoothie in the fridge to cool it down before serving.

Simple Morning Smoothie
Serves 1

Ingredients

½ cucumber, sliced

½ bunch of kale

1 persimmon, sliced

A handful of spinach leaves

½ cup coconut water

Directions

1. Use a high-speed blender and add sliced cucumber, kale, persimmon, spinach leaves, and coconut water to it. Process everything until you get a smooth consistency.
2. You can add some ice or place the smoothie in the fridge to cool it down before serving.

Salads

Alkaline Summer Salad
Serves 2

Ingredients

15 cherry tomatoes

1 carrot

1 beetroot

1 avocado

½ cup quinoa, dry

A handful of basil

A handful of baby peas

A pinch of sage leaves

A pinch of black pepper

A pinch of Himalayan salt (or another healthy salt of your choice)

Olive oil dressing

Directions

1. The first thing you need to do is to prepare the quinoa if you don't have it cooked and drained. Follow the package instructions to make it; it usually involves mixing it with water in a pot, bringing it to a boil and let it simmer until it

absorbs the water. Make sure to drain the quinoa after cooking.

2. Use a grater (or maybe even a spiral slicer) to prepare carrot and beetroot. Once you grate them, transfer them to a serving bowl.

3. Use a pot and add steam baby peas for a couple of minutes to let them cook through. Move them from the heat and leave them for now.

4. Use a knife to slice avocado any way you like (diced pieces are an excellent way to go). Add them to the serving bowl with beetroot and carrot. At this moment, also add sage leaves and basil (chop the herbs if you like).

5. Now, let's prepare the cherry tomatoes. Cut them in half and drizzle with some olive oil. Use a grill or a stove to grill them for about 5 minutes. You want them warmed and just a bit blackened.

6. Once the tomatoes are done, transfer them to the serving bowl and add some black pepper and Himalayan salt, as well as the cooked quinoa. Stir everything to combine the ingredients well. Use olive oil as a dressing to add some extra flavor to your salad (you can use lemon juice instead).

7. Serve immediately or place it in the fridge and save the salad for later.

Alkaline Super Salad
Serves 2

Ingredients

½ red or green pepper, sliced

½ cucumber, sliced

6 cherry tomatoes

A handful of rocket leaves

2 handfuls of baby spinach leaves

A handful of lettuce

A handful of arugula (or kale)

A pack of quinoa, dry

½ cup tofu

1 avocado, sliced

½ can of chickpeas

A handful of nuts and seeds (pumpkin, sunflower, sesame, chia seeds, almonds, walnuts, cashews, or any of your choice)

Salt and pepper to taste

Olive oil

Directions

1. Add some coconut oil to a pan and let it heat over medium temperature. Add the tofu and fry it off lightly for a minute or two.
2. Read the package instructions and prepare the quinoa in accordance with them. It usually involves mixing it with water in a pot, bringing it to a boil and let it simmer until it absorbs the water (no more than 10 minutes). Don't forget to drain any excess liquid after cooking.
3. Wash all the vegetable ingredients (and avocado) thoroughly and chop them any way you see fit at the moment (alternatively, you can simply rip the leaves of the veggies). Use a serving bowl and mix all the ingredients along with the quinoa, tofu and nuts and seeds. Add pepper and salt to your liking and stir everything thoroughly.
4. Serve immediately or place it in the fridge and save the salad for later.

Sprouts Salad Mix
Serves 2

Ingredients

1 onion spring

1 cucumber

A large handful of sprouts (alfalfa, China rose radish or any of your choice)

2 tablespoons coconut oil

½ lemon juice

A handful of fresh parsley, dill, and chives

Salt and pepper to taste

Directions

1. Use a knife and chop dill, chives, and parsley into little pieces. Grab a small bowl and add them to it along with the coconut oil, salt and pepper to taste (make sure to you use a healthy salt), and lemon juice. Mix everything together to make a dressing for the salad.

2. Use a knife to cut cucumber and spring onion into pieces of the desired size. Wash the sprouts thoroughly and drain them.

3. Grab a big serving bowl and pour the dressing into it. Stir once again and then add the cucumber and spring onion, as well as the sprouts. Stir everything to combine the ingredients well.

4. Serve immediately or place it in the fridge and save the salad for later.

Vegetable Salad with Kohlrabi
Serves 2

Ingredients

1 spring onion

3 green kohlrabi, peeled and sliced

4 tablespoons sprouts, fresh (radish sprouts, alfalfa or any of your liking)

3 tablespoons olive oil

½ lemon juice

Salt and pepper to taste

Directions

1. Use a knife to slice the spring onion into pieces of the desired size. Grab a bowl and add sprouts, lemon juice, olive oil, and salt and pepper to taste to it (make sure to use a healthy salt option). Stir everything to combine the ingredients well. Add the cut onion to the mixture and mix everything once again.
2. Use a peeler to peel the kohlrabi and then slice it into pieces of the desired size (I suggest thin slices). Lay the pieces of kohlrabi on a big serving plate. Pour the dressing over the kohlrabi.
3. Serve immediately or place it in the fridge and save the salad for later.

Avocado Salad Mix
Serves 2

Ingredients

2 handfuls of spinach leaves, fresh

1 tomato

1 avocado

2 handfuls of lettuce (any green lettuce of your choice, such as lambs)

11 almonds

1 onion

1 garlic clove

2 carrots, grated

2 tablespoons olive oil

1 lime juice

Salt and pepper to taste

Directions

1. Wash spinach leaves and green lettuce thoroughly. Grab a big serving bowl and add them to it along with grated carrots. Stir to combine all the ingredients well.

2. Use a knife to cut the tomato, garlic, onion, and avocado into pieces of the desired size (the smaller, the better). Grab another bowl and add the pieces to it. Use a fork to mash the ingredients thoroughly. Your goal is to get a puree-like consistency. Add lime juice and olive oil and stir to combine everything together.

3. The next step is to pour the puree you made over the carrot-spinach mixture that's already in the serving bowl. Use a knife to cut the almonds into tiny pieces and add them to the bowl. Stir everything to combine the ingredients well.

4. Add salt and pepper to adjust the taste of your salad (make sure to use a healthy salt option). Stir everything again.

5. Serve immediately or place it in the fridge and save the salad for later.

Warm Alkaline Broccoli Salad
Serves 2

Ingredients

½ cup cherry tomatoes, sliced

1 2/3 cup broccoli, fresh, cut into florets

2 tablespoons chopped parsley, fresh

1 onion, sliced

2 teaspoons dried thyme and oregano

1 tablespoon olive oil

1 lemon juice

Salt and pepper to taste

Directions

1. Follow the list of ingredients and prepare everything as listed above (make sure to use a healthy salt option, such as Himalayan).
2. Grab a frying pan and add florets of broccoli to it. Steam them for a couple of minutes until they become intensely green (you want them to keep their crunchy texture).
3. Grab a big salad bowl and add broccoli, sliced onion, and cherry tomatoes to it. Use olive oil and lemon juice as a dressing and add dried thyme and oregano and chopped fresh parsley. Use salt and pepper to adjust the taste. Stir everything to combine the ingredients well.
4. Serve immediately or place it in the fridge and save the salad for later.

Alkaline Quinoa Salad
Serves 2

Ingredients

3 tomatoes, finely sliced and seeded

1 avocado, sliced into quarters

1 ½ cups quinoa

1 cucumber, peeled and diced

1 red onion, finely chopped

A handful of chopped parsley, fresh

½ cup of pine nuts

3 tablespoons lemon juice, fresh

¼ cup olive oil

2 teaspoons lemon zest, grated

Salt and pepper to taste

Directions

1. Use a medium pot and water to it. Bring it to a boil and add the quinoa. Place the lid over the pot and reduce the temperature to low-medium. Allow it to simmer for about 15-20 minutes (you will know it's done when the quinoa gets tender). Make sure to drain the quinoa once it is done.

2. Turn the oven to 375F to preheat it. Use a baking tray and arrange pine nuts on it. Bake them for about 4 minutes until you brown them a bit. Allow it to cool down. Once cooled, transfer to a big salad bowl.

3. Add the cooked and drained quinoa to the bowl along with tomatoes, parsley, cucumber, and onion. Stir everything to combine the ingredients.

4. Use lemon juice, lemon zest, and olive oil to drizzle the salad. Use salt and pepper to adjust the taste to your liking. Stir everything well to combine the ingredients. Arrange avocado quarters on top of the salad for garnish.

5. Serve immediately or place it in the fridge and save the salad for later.

Lettuce Salad
Serves 2

Ingredients

8 romaine lettuce leaves (or any of your choice that make good lettuce cups)

¼ cup red onion, minced

1 can of Adzuki beans (15 ounces), rinsed and drained

1 lime

1 avocado

A handful of chopped cilantro

Salt and pepper to taste

Directions

1. Drain and rinse the Adzuki beans and add them to a bowl along with the minced red onion. Use a fork to mash everything until you get a puree-like consistency. Add the cilantro and stir to combine the ingredients.
2. Make the cups out of the lettuce and insert the puree into them (use a spoon). Use the lime to make juice out of it and pour it over the mixture. Cut the avocado into the slices of the desired size and top the puree with it. Use salt and pepper to adjust the taste to your liking (if you like, you can also add some red pepper flakes).
3. Serve immediately.

Soups

Tuscan Bean Soup
Serves 6

Ingredients

6 cups cannellini beans, tinned

3 cups tomatoes, chopped

1 carrot, chopped

½ cup quinoa

1 onion, chopped

4 garlic cloves, chopped

2 celery stalks, chopped

¼ cup chopped basil leaves, fresh

5 cups water

2 tablespoons olive oil

Salt and pepper to taste

Directions

1. Use a big pan and add several spoons of water to it. Add the chopped onion, garlic, and celery and steam until it becomes tender (it shouldn't take more than a couple of minutes). Add the chopped carrot and tomatoes and turn the temperature to medium-low. Allow everything to cook for approximately 15-20 minutes.
2. The next step is to add the cannellini beans from the tin along with the water. At this point, you should also add salt and pepper to adjust the taste to your liking (make sure to use a healthy option for salt, such as Himalayan). Stir everything and cook for approximately 20 minutes or until the beans become soft and tender.
3. The final move is adding the quinoa to the pan and cooking for additional 10 minutes or until it becomes al dente.
4. Allow the soup to cool down for a couple of minutes and then add chopped basil leaves and the olive oil. Stir everything and serve while it's warm.

Healthy Alkaline Soup
Serves 4

Ingredients

2 cups kale, chopped

3 stalks celery, cut into dices

2 garlic cloves, minced

½ red onion cut into dices

6 cups vegetable stock

3 carrots cut into dices

1 cup tomatoes, chopped

1 broccoli cut into florets

½ zucchini cut into slices

1 tablespoon fresh ginger, minced

¼ teaspoon cayenne pepper

1 teaspoon turmeric, minced

1 lemon juice

1 tablespoon coconut oil

Salt and pepper to taste

Directions

1. Use a big pot and add coconut oil to it. Heat it over medium temperature and add garlic and onion you previously minced and diced. Sauté them for approximately 5 minutes in the pan before adding carrots and celery. After that, make sure to sauté for another 4-5 minutes.

2. Add tomatoes, broccoli, and minced ginger. Take a look at the clock and sauté for an extra 5 minutes. The next things to insert are cayenne pepper and turmeric. At this point, you should also add salt and pepper to adjust the taste to your liking (make sure to use a healthy option for salt, such as Himalayan). Finally, add vegetable stock and stir the ingredients in the pot.

3. Bring everything to a boil and then reduce the temperature to medium-low and allow the soup to simmer for approximately 10 minutes. Add lemon juice and kale and simmer for another 7-8 minutes.

4. Transfer to serving bowls and serve while it is hot.

Soothing Soup
Serves 4

Ingredients

1 can of lentils (about 1 cup), washed and drained

1 big sweet potato

2 carrots

A generous handful of spinach

1 avocado

4 garlic cloves

2 tablespoons chopped dill

1 red bell pepper

A handful of chopped cashews

1 brown onion

1 cup of vegetable stock

1 tablespoon coconut oil

Directions

1. The first thing to do is to wash and drain the lentils. Set them aside for now once you prepare them.
2. Use a knife to chop the garlic and onion roughly. Grab a big saucepan and add coconut oil to it. Heat it over medium temperature and

add onion and garlic. Allow it to brown for a couple of minutes.

3. In the meantime, peel the sweet potato and carrots and chop them with your knife. Once you finish cutting, through the carrots and potato into the pan and combine to make sure that the ingredients are well mixed and coated in oil. Stir constantly for approximately 2 minutes because you want the carrots and potato to get the flavors from onion and garlic.

4. Add vegetable stock to the pan and allow everything to simmer for approximately 10 minutes. Your goal is to gently cook the vegetables (make sure you don't overcook them). Now, add the lentils and allow the soup to simmer for another 5 minutes.

5. Stir and transfer everything to a food processor or a blender (you might have to do this in a couple of batches). Roughly slice the avocado, dill, and spinach and add them to the blender, too. Deseed and roughly chop the red bell pepper and also throw it into the blender. Process all the ingredients until you get a smooth consistency.

6. Use chopped cashews for garnish or use olive oil to drizzle the soup if you like it that way. Transfer to serving bowls and serve while it is warm.

Cold Avocado Soup
Serves 1

Ingredients

3 avocados cut into dices

1 cup cucumber cut into dices

2 scallions

2 lemons, squeezed

2 cups watercress

Cherry tomatoes cut in halves

Salt and pepper to taste

1 ½ cups of water (you can use alkaline, but it's not mandatory)

Directions

1. Use a blender or a food processor and add sliced avocados, cucumber, scallions, watercress, and water to it. Squeeze the juice from two lemons and add it to the blender, too. Process everything until you get a soup-like consistency.
2. Add salt and pepper to adjust the taste to your liking (make sure to use a healthy option for salt, such as Himalayan). Stir everything well and use cherry tomatoes for garnish.
3. Serve immediately or place it in the fridge to cool down.

Lentil Soup with Herbs
Serves 4

Ingredients

4 cloves garlic, minced

1 onion, chopped into small pieces

2 carrots cut into pieces

1 ½ cups brown lentils, rinsed

6 cups vegetable stock (or broth)

2 celery stalks cut into pieces

1 teaspoon thyme

1 bay leaf

A handful of chopped parsley

1 tablespoon olive oil

Salt and pepper to taste

Directions

1. Use a large pot and add olive oil to it. Heat it over medium temperature. Once heated, add the chopped onions and sauté for about 4 minutes or until they become translucent (make sure that you occasionally stir to prevent burning).

2. Add celery, carrots, and garlic and sauté for approximately 3 minutes, while stirring occasionally. Add the vegetable stock (or broth), bay leaf, lentils, and thyme. At this point, you should also add salt and pepper to adjust the taste to your liking (make sure to use a healthy option for salt, such as Himalayan). Stir everything to combine the ingredients well. Reduce the temperature to medium-low and allow everything to cook for approximately 35 minutes.

3. Add chopped parsley and stir the ingredients once again. Transfer to serving bowls and serve while it's warm.

Simple Fennel Soup
Serves 2

Ingredients

1 cup vegetable stock (or broth)

½ teaspoon flax seed oil

2 fennel bulbs

1 teaspoon orange zest, grated

4 tablespoons lemon juice, fresh

2 tablespoons orange juice, fresh

1 teaspoon ground coriander

Pepper to taste

Directions

1. The first thing you need to do is to prepare the fennel bulbs. Clean them first and then cut the stalks out. Slice them into pieces that are very thin and make sure to keep the fennel leaves for garnish.
2. Use a large pot and add freshly squeezed orange juice and vegetable stock to it. Bring it to a boil. Insert the fennel and cook for approximately 12-15 minutes over medium-low temperature. Your goal is to get the fennel soft.
3. Transfer the mixture from the pot into a high-speed blender. Process it for a couple of seconds until you get a puree-like consistency.
4. Use ground coriander, freshly squeezed orange juice, flax seed oil, and pepper to adjust the taste to your liking. Use the orange zest and fennel leaves for garnish and serve immediately.

Entrees

Alkaline Stir Fry
Serves 2

Ingredients

1-inch piece chopped ginger

1 onion cut into small pieces

½ a squash cut into small pieces, deseeded

¼ green cabbage (or any other cabbage you like)

1 green or red chili, chopped

3 handfuls of leafy greens, chopped (use Swiss chard, spinach, kale, etc.)

2 garlic cloves, chopped

½ lemon juice, fresh

2 tablespoons coconut oil

Salt and pepper to taste

Directions

1. Use a large pan and add coconut oil to it. Heat it over medium temperature. Once it is heated, add onion to it and reduce the heat to medium-low. Fry the onion for a couple of minutes until it becomes fragrant; add chili, ginger, and garlic at that point. Continue cooking for an additional minute and make sure to stir constantly because you don't want to overcook the garlic or it will become bitter.
2. Add a pinch of salt (make sure to use a healthy option for salt, such as Himalayan) and squash to the pan. Fry for a minute or two until you notice that the squash is becoming tender.
3. Add the combination of leafy greens of your choice. Squeeze the lemon juice and insert it into the pan as well. If needed, add extra salt and some pepper to adjust the seasoning. Cook for about 2 minutes, no more than that, as it is the best way to keep the flavor, nutrients, and freshness of the leafy greens.
4. Transfer to serving plates and serve immediately.

Cauliflower 'Wings' with Domestic Barbecue Sauce

Serves 2

Ingredients

1 teaspoon garlic powder

1 cup of garbanzo flour

1 head of cauliflower, cut into small pieces

1 cup of water

Domestic Barbecue Sauce to taste

Salt to taste

Domestic Barbecue Sauce:

2 cloves garlic, crushed

1 brown onion, grated

1 teaspoon ground allspice

1 teaspoon ground cumin

1 teaspoon coriander

1 tablespoon coconut oil

1 tablespoon Worcestershire sauce

1 tablespoon Dijon mustard

1/3 cup tomato sauce (organic)

½ teaspoon cayenne pepper

1 teaspoon lemon juice

Directions

1. The first thing we need to do is to prepare the barbecue sauce. Use a saucepan and add coconut oil to it. Heat the oil over low temperature. Once it is heated, add garlic, onion, cumin, coriander, cayenne pepper, and allspice. Stir everything together and cook for approximately 5 minutes.
2. Squeeze the lemon juice and cook for approximately another minute. Next, add Dijon mustard, Worcestershire sauce, and organic tomato sauce along with a cup of water to the mix.
3. Adjust the temperature to medium. Add salt and pepper to adjust the taste to your liking (make sure to use a healthy option for salt, such as Himalayan). Once the sauce is close to a boil, reduce the heat to medium-low and allow it to simmer for approximately 12 minutes.
4. The idea is to enable the sauce to thicken a bit. Once this happens, transfer it to a high-speed blender. Process all the ingredients until you get a smooth consistency and you've got yourself a domestic barbecue sauce.

5. Now, let's move on to preparing the cauliflower 'wings.' First, turn your oven to 450F to preheat it. While it's preheating, grab a bowl and add garbanzo flour, garlic powder, and water to it. Salt to your taste (once again, make sure it's a healthy salt option). Whisk everything until you get a consistency that reminds of batter.
6. Add the cauliflower to the mix and toss everything together. Arrange on a baking tray and place it into the oven. Bake for approximately 20 minutes, but make sure to flip them after 10.
7. Transfer to serving bowls and serve the domestic barbecue sauce as a dip.

Zucchini Pasta with Lemon Spinach Pesto
Serves 2

Ingredients

3 cups baby spinach

3 cloves garlic

4 zucchinis

¼ cup basil

½ cup cherry tomatoes halved

1 lemon juice

½ cup olive oil

¼ cup cashews

Salt and pepper to taste

Directions

1. The first thing to do is to cut the zucchini into long pieces (you can use a grater or a spiral cutter to do this). If you prefer it a bit softer, you can sauté the zucchini for approximately 2 minutes with some coconut oil in your saucepan before cutting it.

2. Use a high-speed blender or a food processor and add baby spinach, garlic, basil, and cashews to it. Process everything until you combine the ingredients well. Gradually add lemon juice and olive oil to the mix and stir to combine everything together. Add salt and pepper to adjust the taste to your liking (make sure to use a healthy option for salt, such as Himalayan) and stir once again.

3. Use a serving bowl and add the zucchini and pesto to it. Toss the ingredients together well and use cherry tomatoes to garnish the pasta. Serve immediately.

Winter Pasta with Kelp Noodles
Serves 4

Ingredients

3 garlic cloves, minced

1 broccoli head, medium

1 leek cut into thin slices

1 can of garbanzo beans

1 pack of kelp noodles

3 tablespoons olive oil

½ teaspoon red pepper flakes

A sprig of rosemary, chopped

A handful of parsley, chopped

Salt and pepper to taste

Directions

1. Turn your oven to 400F to preheat it. Use a bowl and add broccoli, garlic, olive oil, red pepper flakes, and salt to taste (make sure to use a healthy option for salt, such as Himalayan). Toss everything together and bake for about 20 minutes. You want to make the broccoli tender, so you can get it out once it achieves this state.

2. Grab kelp noodles and rinse and drain them. Use a pot and add hot water to it. Soak the noodles in that water.

3. Use a saucepan and add olive oil to it. Heat it over medium temperature. Once it is heated, add leeks and cook them for approximately 8 minutes or until they are melted.

4. In the meantime, drain the noodles. Once the leeks are melted, add the noodle to the pan and cook for additional 8 minutes.

5. Transfer the broccoli to the pan once it is roasted. Add rosemary, parsley, and more salt and pepper to adjust the taste to your liking. Also, add a can of garbanzo beans and stir everything together. Transfer to serving bowls and serve immediately.

6. Tip: You don't have to use garbanzo beans if you are looking for a more alkaline recipe. However, they are a good source of protein if that fits your nutrition plan at that moment.

Kale Chickpea Rolls with salsa
Serves 4

Ingredients

12 big kale leaves

¾ cup vegetable stock (or broth)

1 teaspoon ground cumin

½ teaspoon ground paprika

½ cup brown rice (basmati or any other of your choice)

1 cup chickpeas, cooked

1 onion cut into small pieces

1 teaspoon olive oil

Salt to taste

Salsa:

3 jalapeno peppers

1 can of organic plum tomatoes

1 onion

A bunch of coriander

Directions

1. Use a saucepan and add olive oil to it. Heat it over medium temperature. Once it is heated, add the onion and cook them for approximately 4 minutes or until they become soft. Add vegetable stock, brown rice, cumin, paprika, and chickpeas (make sure that they are cooked). Stir and bring everything to a boil.

2. Once it boils reduce the temperature to medium-low, stir and allow the mixture to simmer for approximately 15 minutes or until you see that all the liquid is absorbed. Take it off the heat and let it cool down.

3. In the meantime, you can make the salsa in your high-speed blender or a food processor (if you must, use a hand mixer). Add the plum onions to the bottom of the blender. Use your knife to peel the onion and slice it into quarters. Arrange the onions over the tomatoes. Cut off the stems from the coriander and jalapeno peppers (don't forget to wash and drain them first) and add them to the mix. Please note that you can adjust the amount of jalapenos depending on how spicy you prefer your salsa. Cover the blender with a lid and process the ingredients for about 45 seconds. You want to blend all the ingredients, but not too much because you don't want the salsa to thicken. Set the salsa aside for now.

4. Grab kale leaves and wash them thoroughly. After draining them, cut the thick stems you find in the middle of the leaves. Arrange 1 big leaf (or 2 small ones) on your kitchen counter or any available area. Pull together the edges where you removed the stem to overlap.

5. Add approximately 2 tablespoons of the rice-chickpea mixture and pour it over the bottom of the leaf. Roll up the leaf to the tip and fold in the sides. Do the same with the remaining leaves until you use all of them, or there is no more filling.

6. Arrange the kale rolls on a serving plate and top it with the salsa before serving.

Alkaline Vegetable Stew
Serves 2

Ingredients

1 cup chickpeas

2 new potatoes

3 big onions

1 courgette

1 red or yellow pepper

1 red chili, fresh

3 tablespoons sesame oil

A pinch of ground cardamom

A pinch of ground ginger

A pinch of ground coriander

A pinch of ground cumin

3 tablespoons sesame oil

Salt and pepper to taste

Directions

1. Use a pot with some cold water to soak the chickpeas. If you have the option, you can leave them overnight, but make sure to leave them for at least an hour.

2. Add some more cold water to the pot (to approximately double the amount) and cook the chickpeas for about 60 minutes.

3. Use a knife to peel the onions and slice them into rings. Grab the potatoes, wash them thoroughly and peel them before cutting them into bite-sized pieces. Do the same with the carrots and the courgette. Red pepper also needs to be washed, deseeded and sliced into rings. Finally, deseed the chili and slice it into small pieces.

4. Use a big pan and add sesame oil to it. Heat it over medium temperature. Once it is heated, add the onions to it and fry for a minute or two until it becomes fragrant. Add red pepper, cumin, chili, coriander, cardamom, ginger, and salt (make sure that you choose a healthy salt option, such as Himalayan). Stir constantly and fry for a minute or two.

5. Next, add courgette, carrots, and potato and fry for additional 45 seconds. Make sure to stir constantly to prevent from burning. You can add a cup of water to help you to scrape everything from the sides and the bottom of the pan.

6. Drain the chickpeas you previously cooked and add them to the stew. At the very end, add another cup of water and stir everything. Serve while it's warm.

Desserts

Blackberry Parfait
Serves 1

Ingredients

1/3 cup gluten-free rolled oats

1 cup frozen blackberries (or any other berries of your choice)

½ teaspoon vanilla extract

½ cup of unsweetened coconut milk (you can use almond milk instead)

½ cup cashews, soaked

1 tablespoon hemp seeds

Directions

1. Soak the cashews in a cup of water and allow them to sit for at least 20 minutes (preferably an hour).
2. Use a food processor or a blender and add cashews, vanilla extract, and coconut milk to it. Process the ingredients until you get a creamy consistency.
3. Grab a serving cup and arrange cashew cream on the bottom of it. Add berries to it and place some oats on top. Finally, garnish with hemp seeds. Put it in the fridge to cool down or serve immediately.

Strawberry Ice Cream
Serves 4

Ingredients

1 cup coconut milk (you can use almond milk instead)

2 frozen bananas

½ cup strawberries (frozen or fresh)

1 tablespoon hemp seeds

1 tablespoon goji berries

2 tablespoons coconut flakes, unsweetened

2 teaspoons chia seeds

2 cups ice

Directions

1. Use a food processor or a blender and add coconut milk, chia seeds, bananas, strawberries, and ice to it. Blend everything until you get a smooth consistency.
2. Add goji berries and process everything once again (there can be traces of berries left). Use hemp seeds and coconut flakes to sprinkle the ice cream. Place it in the freezer for at least an hour to firm. Serve chilled.

Raw Pumpkin Pie
Serves 6

Ingredients

12 ounces organic pumpkin puree (1 ¼ cup)

1 cup pecans, soaked

½ teaspoon nutmeg

½ teaspoon cinnamon

1 teaspoon of vanilla

6 dates

Salt to taste

Crust:

1 cup dates

1 cup coconut flakes, unsweetened

1 cup almonds, raw

1 teaspoon cinnamon

Directions

1. Use a food processor or a blender and add raw almonds, unsweetened coconut flakes, and cinnamon to it (all the crust ingredients). Process everything until you notice that it starts sticking together. Use a pie pan and transfer the crust into it (don't forget to mold against the sides to make sure the crust sticks).
2. Now, let' make the filling. Wash and wipe your blender and add pecans, dates, nutmeg, cinnamon, pumpkin puree, and salt to taste (make sure to use a healthy salt option, such as Himalayan salt) to it. Process everything until you blend the ingredients together.
3. Transfer the filling to the pan with the pie crust. If you want, you can use some additional cinnamon to sprinkle the pie. Put it in the fridge to cool down for at least an hour.
4. Tip: Before starting to prepare the pie, soak the pecans in a pot of cold water and let them sit for at least 20 minutes or up to an hour.

Avocado Chocolate Mousse
Serves 1

Ingredients

2/3 cup coconut water

1 ½ avocado, sliced

1 tablespoon vanilla

3 dates

2 tablespoons cacao, raw

1 teaspoon salt

Dark Chocolate chunks for garnish

Directions

1. Use a blender or a food processor and sliced avocado, vanilla, dates, raw cacao, coconut water, and salt to it (make sure to use a healthy salt option, such as Himalayan salt). Process everything until you see a thick consistency.
2. Transfer it to a serving bowl. Use dark chocolate chunks (at least 70% cocoa) to garnish the mousse and place it into the fridge to solidify (it will take about 2 hours). Serve chilled.

Banana Coconut Frozen Yogurt
Serves 2

Ingredients

1 cup coconut milk

2 frozen bananas

1 tablespoon coconut oil

1 scoop of almond butter

4 tablespoons chia seeds

Directions

1. Use a high-speed blender or food processor and add coconut milk, frozen bananas, coconut oil, and almond butter to it. Process the ingredients until you reach the desired consistency.
2. Add chia seeds and decrease the speed of the blender. Process everything for 1 minute at slow speed to keep the seeds whole but still get the most nutrients. You can sprinkle with some cinnamon if you like it that way.
3. Place it in the freezer and allow it to firm for at least an hour. Serve chilled.

Snacks

Alkaline Energy Balls
Serves 12 balls

Ingredients

1 cup almond meal

4 dates

1/3 cup cacao powder

¼ cup almonds

1/3 cup pistachios

½ cup coconut, shredded

1 tablespoon chia seeds

1/3 cup coconut oil

Directions

1. The first thing to do is to remove the seed from the dates. Next, use a high-speed blender or a food processor and add almond meal, dates, half of the pistachios, coconut oil, almonds, shredded coconut, chia seeds, and cocoa powder to it. Process the ingredients until you blend everything well.
2. Transfer the mixture to a bowl and allow it to sit for several minutes. In the meantime, smash the half of the pistachios remaining.
3. Make the balls out of the almonds mixture and coat by rolling them in the pistachios. Arrange on a serving plate.

Alkaline Snack Wrap
Serves 2

Ingredients

2 tomatoes, ripe

6 large lettuce leaves (iceberg or romaine)

½ of chili, fresh

½ red onion

3 avocados, ripe

1 lemon juice

A pinch of salt

A bunch of fresh parsley and coriander

Directions

1. Put the avocados into a bowl and use a fork to mash them. Next, use your knife to chop the onion, tomatoes, parsley, and coriander. Make sure you cut everything into small pieces.
2. Now, add the squeezed juice from 1 lemon to the avocado bowl and sprinkle with a bit of salt (make sure to use a healthy salt option, such as Himalayan). Add onion, tomatoes, parsley, and coriander and mix everything together.
3. Wash and dry the lettuce leaves and arrange them on the kitchen counter. Proportionally divide the mixture from the bowl across the leaves. Wrap them and use cocktail sticks to make sure they hold.
4. Serve immediately.

Kale Chips
Serves 2

Ingredients

1 tablespoon olive oil

1 teaspoon paprika

A bunch of kale

A pinch of salt

Dried chili flakes (optional)

Directions

1. Turn your oven to 400F to preheat it. While it's preheating, rip the kale to make chips out of it (you should make 1 or 2-inch squares).
2. Use your hands to toss the kale chips in salt and olive oil (make sure that you use a healthy option for the salt, such as Himalayan).
3. Arrange the kale chips on a baking dish and place them in the oven for approximately 10 minutes. Before serving, sprinkle with some paprika. If you want it spicier, also sprinkle with dried chili flakes.

Coconut Chia Cream Pots
Serves 4

Ingredients

1 cup coconut yogurt

1 cup coconut milk

1 date

¼ cup chia seeds

1 teaspoon sesame seeds

1 tablespoon flax seeds

½ teaspoon vanilla extract

Directions

1. Deseed the dates and add them to a high-speed blender or a food processor along with coconut milk. Process them until you blend the ingredients together.
2. Transfer the milk to a big bowl and add vanilla extract, chia seeds, sesame seeds, and flax seeds. Combine all the ingredients together well. Place the mixture in the refrigerator for approximately 30 minutes.
3. When you want to serve, prepare a pot and add a layer of coconut yogurt on the bottom. Next, add the seed mix from the fridge and top it with some more coconut yogurt.
4. If you want, you can sprinkle with some additional nuts.

Conclusion

Thank you again for purchasing this book!

I hope this book was able to help you prepare some delicious food to fit into your alkaline diet.

As you can see, all the alkaline recipes in this book are extremely healthy. I tried to cover all parts of the day, and I hope you like all recipes, including breakfast, lunch, dinner, snacks, and sweets. All of the recipes were personally tested by me, and I believe that they are perfect for all people who love alkaline food.

Finally, if you enjoyed this book, then I'd like to ask you for a favor, would you be kind enough to leave a review for this book on Amazon? It'd be greatly appreciated.

Visit the link below to leave a review:
https://www.amazon.com/review/create-review
For more information, please check out my blog at:
Mastering-life.com

Thank you and good luck!

Preview Of
"Alkaline Diet" Book

Introduction

I want to thank you and congratulate you for Purchasing the book "**Alkaline Diet!**"

We can see that there are so many diets available to us. Each diet has its benefits, but each also comes with its downsides. Now, when you think about different diets and choosing the ideal one for you, the word balance comes to your mind. If you are looking for a diet offering you the perfect balance, it's the alkaline diet.

We will talk later about how this diet works, but the important thing to know is that it keeps pH levels throughout your body balanced. That, in turn, secured that your organism reaches the optimum state and, therefore, optimum health. Aside from being able to help you get your weight in order, alkaline diet will assist you in dealing with some annoying health issues, such as chronic pain and other illnesses.

The book in front of you will cover the following:

- **What is alkaline diet and how it works** – explaining the principles of eating alkaline-promoting food and properly keeping the acid-alkaline balance in your body
- **How to check your acidic levels** – higher levels of acid may cause numerous health problems. Fortunately, it's easy to keep track of your acidic levels if you follow the simple directions in this book
- **Health benefits and risks of the alkaline diet** – the alkaline style of life has numerous advantages for both physical and mental health, but the most important benefit is that it provides an entirely natural way to lose extra pounds and MAINTAIN them. We will also cover some risks of the diet to make sure everything goes the way it should.
- **Mistakes beginners often make** – my goal is to show you how to apply the alkaline diet concept to your life successfully. The best way to do that is to analyze what mistakes beginners often make so that you can learn from them
- **Foods to eat and avoid** – each diet has its go-to foods that are a must and the foods that you should make sure to avoid. The "Alkaline Diet" book will recommend you which foods you should consume and which you should avoid, as well as offer some tips on how to combine your food. Another mystery that we will solve is whether you should drink alkaline water during your diet.

And much more!

Whether you are looking for a way to lose extra pounds or you want to get your health back on track, the alkaline diet is the right way to go. Everything you need to know about this way of nutrition is located in one place – here.

Thanks again for downloading this book, I hope you enjoy it!

What Is Alkaline Diet
& How It Works

You might have heard about alkaline diet before, but you can't quite define it. The alkaline diet is related to the pH level of blood, urine, and other fluids in your body. The goal of the alkaline diet is to balance these pH levels.

The food you eat partially determines these levels through its mineral density. All forms of life on Earth need to keep their pH to maintain their health. In fact, various experts suggest that there is no chance for any disease to develop if a person has a balanced pH in his/her body.

You will find different opinions when it comes to the connection of pH levels and diseases and disorders, but there is one thing all scientists agree on. Humans should have a certain pH ratio of the blood that's 'perfect' for their body. That ratio should be anywhere between 7.2 and 7.4. Your body always aims towards this ideal pH amount. In fact, it sometimes goes to extraordinary lengths to keep the ratio in the appropriate and safe boundaries.

Depending on the time of the day, your way of nutrition, what you had for your last meal and when you most recently went to the bathroom, your pH levels will vary. That is why diet is imperative. If you often consume a lot of highly acidic foods, there is a chance that your body's pH level will change and lead to a state called "acidosis." The imbalance of electrolytes can also cause acidosis to develop.

What Are pH Levels and Why Are They Important?

The abbreviation pH I have already mentioned a couple of times is short for the potential of hydrogen. That is what measures the alkalinity or the acidity of our body. There is a pH scale used for measurement, and it goes from 0 to 14. A lower number marks highly acidic food while higher numbers mean that something is more alkaline. Considering this scale, we can conclude that a pH level of 7 is considered as neutral. However, if you take into account that the most appropriate pH for a human body is around 7.3, you come to a conclusion that the best thing to do is to keep your organism slightly alkaline. You should also know that pH levels are different in various parts of your body. The stomach is the section that tends to be the most acidic.

Go to this link to check out the rest of the "**Alkaline Diet V.1**" Book:

http://amzn.to/2shity1

Check Out My Other Books

Below you'll find some of my other popular books that are popular on Amazon and Kindle as well. Simply click on the links below to check them out.

Alternatively, you can visit my "Author Page" on Amazon to see other work done by me:

Anas Malla: http://amzn.to/2nzCevB

- **Alkaline Diet V.1**
  http://amzn.to/2shityl

- **Ketogenic Diet**
  http://amzn.to/2ps3ePm

- **Ketogenic Bread Cookbook V.1**
  http://amzn.to/2m8hixm

- **Ketogenic Bread Cookbook V.2**
  http://amzn.to/2r3qsPJ

- **Ketogenic Bread Cookbook V.3**
  http://amzn.to/2r3Af8j

- **Instant Pot Ketogenic Cookbook V.1**
  http://amzn.to/2o4oCfP

- **Instant Pot Ketogenic Cookbook V.2**
  http://amzn.to/2o4oCfP

- **Ketogenic Fat Bombs V.1**
  http://amzn.to/2qDgS4U

- **Minimalist Living**
  http://amzn.to/2phTu8M

- **Conversation Tactics**
  http://amzn.to/2oj23Qg

If the links do not work, for whatever reason, you can simply search for these titles on the Amazon website to find them.